Ever New

A SELF CARE JOURNAL TO HELP YOU LEARN, UNLEARN, & HEAL.

Deneil Foster

A SELF CARE JOURNAL TO HELP YOU LEARN, UNLEARN, & HEAL.
Copyright © 2022 Deneil Foster

All rights reserved.

Although the author has made every effort to ensure that the information in this book was correct at press time, the author does not assume and hereby disclaim any liability to any party for any loss, damage, or disruption caused by errors or omissions, whether such errors or omissions result from negligence, accident, or any other cause.

No parts of this book may be reproduced in any form or by any electronic or mechanical means, including information storage in retrieval systems, without written permission from the author, except in the case of a reviewer, who may quote
brief passages embodied in critical articles or in a review.

Edited By: Crystal S. Wright

ISBN: 978-1-7378345-5-7

10 9 8 7 6 5 4 3 2 1
Printed in the United States

Priceless Publishing®
pricelesspublishing.co
Lauderhill, Florida

THIS SELF-CARE JOURNAL BELONGS TO

_____

DATE

_____

Contents

Author's Note | **1**
Guidelines on Use | **3**

SECTION 1 - BACK TO THE BEGINNING

Acknowledging The Root | **6**

SECTION 2 - INNER HEALING

The Inner Child | **13**
When You've Hit Rock Bottom | **50**
Forgiveness | **63**

SECTION 3 - CREATE THE LIFE YOU WANT

Reprogramming Your Mind | **74**
Manifestations | **90**
Goals | **96**
Building Healthy Relationships | **111**
Health: Mental, Physical & Financial | **142**

SECTION 4 - MAINTAINING THE GAINS

Self-Love & Self Care | **174**
Coping Skills | **191**
Staying True To Yourself | **197**
Reflection | **209**

Epilogue | **212**
Free Resources | **213**
End Notes | **214**

Author's Note

I am an only child raised by a Jamaican, Christian, single mom. Though there were times when my mom struggled to provide for me, she always aimed to be the best mother possible, and made sure I had a memorable childhood.

As I grew older, things took a bad turn. My mom went on a venture to get closer to God and everything changed. As she got closer to God, she became very strict. I felt like I was robbed of my joy, peace, freedom, and experiences. I was no longer allowed to participate in the activities that had previously brought joy to my life, and I felt like I wasn't allowed to make any mistakes. My mom and the Church were now in control of my thoughts and actions. I was living the life that they wanted for me and not one I envisioned for myself.

All this severely impacted my mental health. I didn't get the freedom to figure out who I was or where I fit in the world. As a result of this, when I transitioned into adulthood, I was adulting all wrong. I didn't trust myself. I always sought validation and approval from others. I always did what others said to do or said was best. I wasn't confident. Being an only child and a depressed one at that, I feared being alone. This caused me to become a codependent people pleaser. I was always trying to help or fix someone when the person who needed it most was me.

I tried to convince myself that things weren't that bad but I would say worrisome things like, *"shoot me in the face"* for the smallest reasons, such as a car cutting me off or getting anything less than the perfect score on a test. I didn't even realize the words coming out of my mouth. That goes to show how out of touch I was with myself.

From the outside looking in, I was happy, strong and confident. Inside I was broken, scared, and alone. I was angry with my Mom. I was angry with the Church. I was angry with myself. I was angry with friends. I was angry with God. I had no self-love or self-awareness, so I externalized my pain. Carrying around anger and self-doubt is not easy. It reached a point where as much as I wanted to pour into others, I had nothing left in my cup. I was empty. And that's when I knew, something had to change, and quick.

I went on a search to find a therapist and was pleased when I finally found one who I connected well with. In therapy I learned so much about myself and how health and happiness really look. I had so much unlearning to do. I was conditioned to act and think a certain way. Anything outside of that was a disgrace or a disappointment. This caused me to judge myself and others so harsh.

I took a step back from the people, around me and decided to love on myself and be myself. I became my own friend, my biggest supporter, my right-hand man. I learned how to follow my heart. I learned how to think positive and manifest. I learned how to value myself. I learned that I'm allowed to make mistakes and grow through life. I learned how to find beauty in my imperfections.

I've gained so much confidence, independence, and happiness. I've learned to love myself in the purest and most authentic form. I've learned to cheer myself on when no one else is in the bleachers. I've learned to forgive the 'unforgivable'. I've learned to trust myself and trust my process. Through all this, it has created inner peace. This inner peace is what we all deserve and is what I want you all to gain from my book.

Guidelines On Use

This journal was designed to help you face the traumas you've endured in your life. You'll be asked a series of questions to help you gain greater awareness and understanding about yourself. This greater knowledge and understanding of yourself will help you to attain the purest, most authentic form of self-love. You'll begin to unlearn the teachings that no longer serve you and learn about the ones that do.

All I ask is this: as you face each topic, be 100% honest with yourself. Release all your emotions and thoughts on the pages as you work through the journal, because yes — this is work. But if you do it right it will be the most rewarding work you'll ever do.

With the proper usage, this book will help you blossom into your most healed, loved, aware and rejuvenated self.

**Get your pen out, your beverage of choice
and a box of Kleenex because things are about to get real!**

Say This Aloud:

I have embarked on a journey towards a stronger, healthier, more loving, and forgiving version of myself.

Every day I learn, unlearn and heal.

As I journey through life, I will cheer myself on every step of the way.

I will become the person I desire to be.

I will receive everything that is meant for me.

I will love myself unconditionally.

Back To The Beginning

"The two most important days in your life are the day you are born and the day you find out why."
Mark Twain.

CHAPTER 1

Acknowledging The Root

A family tree can wither if no one tends to the roots. Let's acknowledge your root.

When were you born?

_____
_____

Where were you born?

_____
_____

What is your ethnicity and nationality?

_____
_____

Is your family religious or non-religious?

_____
_____

Were you raised in a two-parent home?

_____
_____

What family members were consistent in your life?

_____
_____
_____
_____
_____
_____
_____
_____
_____
_____
_____
_____
_____
_____
_____

Who does your family want you to be?

Are you happy to be a part of the family you were born into? Why or why not?

What generational curse(s) can be found in your family?
(This includes but is not limited to: Abuse of any kind, addiction, diagnosed or undiagnosed mental health illness, divorce, etc.)

_____
_____
_____
_____
_____
_____
_____
_____

What struggles did your family face before you were born?
(For example, homelessness)

_____
_____
_____
_____
_____
_____
_____
_____

Now that you have acknowledged your roots, keep these in mind as you continue your journey. Many obstacles you've faced, may be stemming from your ethnicity, race, religious/non-religious practices, generational curses, and other things that you did not choose but were born into.

Inner Healing

Healing can be painful, but your pain is only temporary. The benefits of healing will last a lifetime.

HURT PEOPLE, HURT PEOPLE.
HEALED PEOPLE, HEAL PEOPLE.
WORK ON YOURSELF SO YOU
CAN WORK ON THE WORLD.

CHAPTER 2
The Inner Child

The inner child is the child-like aspect of ourselves that lives in the subconscious mind. This child-like version of yourself is also known as a sub-personality that presents itself when faced with trauma.

If the inner child is wounded and unhealed, this can cause our mental development to become stagnant. Our mind has the protective ability to keep us at the age we were when the trauma occurred. Our perceptions and reactions in our adult life, often stem from the inner child.

If left unhealed, you will continue to perceive life the same way you did as a child of that age. You will continue to relive the moments where you experienced trauma, and react how you did as a child, or react how you wish you did as a child.

Steps To Healing The Inner Child

1. Acknowledgement
2. Acceptance
3. Apologize & release the pain
4. Reparent

Are you ready to heal your inner child?

_____

_____

Step 1 – Acknowledgement

Knowing what aspects of your childhood carved you into the person you are today will help you maneuver through life. Think back to your childhood. Think about the desires of your younger self. Revisit the moments you experienced joy and pain. If you experienced any trauma in your childhood, that wound needs to be healed.

Many who believe they had a good childhood often neglect their inner child. Your inner child did not need to face trauma in order to show up in your adult life. Whether your childhood has been deemed good or bad, your inner child can continue to subconsciously control your adult life.

How did your family celebrate holidays? (Christmas, birthdays, etc.)

_____
_____
_____
_____
_____
_____
_____

What were you attached to as a child? (A pillow, specific stuffed animal, etc)

_____
_____
_____
_____
_____
_____
_____

What were your families' traditions?

Understanding why you do what you do is just as important as knowing what you do. Many of us picked up unhealthy behavior patterns from our parents, or others in our childhood. Below are possible correlations to the traits associated with the wounded inner child.

Signs that your inner child may be wounded:

- *You self-sabotage*
- *You are co-dependent*
- *You have trust issues*
- *You are materialistic*
- *You are a perfectionist*
- *You fear abandonment*
- *You lack self-discipline*
- *You're very opinionated*
- *You avoid confrontation*
- *You have trouble receiving or accepting love*
- *You are overly independent and tend to refuse help*
- *You are attracted to toxic relationships*
- *You are attracting toxic relationships*
- *You are possessive and clingy with the people and things in your life*
- *You are a people pleaser*

You may **self-sabotage** because growing up your loved ones never spoke highly of you, so now you can't speak highly of yourself.

You may be **co-dependent** because your parents were overly protective, so you never had the chance to explore and learn to stand on your own. Or maybe your parents were more absent or neglectful so now you cling to the people around searching for the support and guidance you never got from your parents.

You may have **trust issues** because you never had consistent people around you. Maybe your parents separated. You possibly faced unfulfilled promises.

You may be **materialistic** because you never received materialistic things growing up. Maybe your family couldn't afford jewelry or new clothes, toys, etc. So now, you try to fill that void with things. Or maybe your parents were materialistic, so you formed this habit of your own.

You may be a **perfectionist** because your family did not accept anything less than perfection from you. Maybe you didn't have the opportunity to learn from mistakes. Maybe you fear rejection due to family rejecting your efforts, so you strive to perfect at all you do to protect yourself.

You may **fear abandonment** because your parents were absent due to work, addiction, separation, or another reason. Your parents probably prioritized many things over you.

You may **lack self-discipline** because you grew up with little or no rules. Maybe your family was quick to speak or act and this culture caused harm. It's possible that your family used aggression or violence to solve problems whether this was used by spanking as a discipline or fighting when you're offended.

You may be **opinionated** because your parents never allowed your opinions to be heard so now you make sure your opinion is heard any and every time. You were probably raised to believe that children must be seen and not heard.

You may **avoid confrontation** because you experienced abuse. This could be verbal or physical abuse. Maybe your parents always pointed out what you did wrong so you lack confidence.

You may **have trouble receiving or accepting love** because you never received it growing up, so it makes you uncomfortable now.

You may be **overly independent** because of having a strict parent. Maybe your family never allowed you to be yourself, so you are making up for it now. Maybe the people in your life were like this so you became the same way. Maybe you grew up in a prideful family that shunned asking for help or receiving handouts.

You may be **attracted to toxic relationships or are attracting toxic relationships** because this seems normal to you. Maybe your parents always fussed and fought. You possibly witnessed someone being abused, then receiving hugs and kisses afterwards by their abuser. Maybe you were the one being abused. Regardless of the reason, you may have been desensitized and have normalized what is toxic.

You may be **possessive and clingy** with people and things in your life because you always had to share. Maybe your parents didn't love on you enough because they catered more to your younger siblings or their significant other. Maybe your family never utilized boundaries, so you tend to overbear. Maybe you were abandoned as a child so now you cling to those around you in hopes that you won't face abandonment.

You may **people please** to seek acceptance. This may make you feel valued. You possibly people please to provide people with what you never received. You may feel like it's an obligation or necessity for you to receive love.

There are so many scenarios that can apply to each, and every trait listed. Find your why!

What traits listed above applies to you? And why do you believe you act this way?

_____
_____
_____
_____
_____
_____
_____
_____
_____
_____

"TURN YOUR WOUNDS INTO WISDOM."
OPRAH WINFREY

Were you neglected by your parents? *Circle one*

YES   NO

Have you experienced abuse? If yes, what kind of abuse? What is it stemming from? How long did this go on?

_____
_____
_____
_____
_____

_____
_____
_____
_____
_____
_____
_____
_____
_____
_____
_____
_____
_____
_____
_____

Were you able to express yourself freely?

_____
_____
_____
_____
_____
_____
_____
_____
_____
_____
_____

Did you feel safe around your family? Why or why not?

_____
_____
_____
_____
_____
_____
_____
_____
_____
_____
_____

Which adjectives would you use to describe your childhood?

Continue to think and reflect on your childhood.

Think about your personality. Think about how you react to certain things. Think about the kind of people you date. Think about the way you speak to your friends and family. Think about the dynamics of your relationships.

Think long, hard, and deep about the events in your life leading up to this point. As you acknowledge your inner child, think about how and why these events made you who you are today.

Use the next few pages to write about your childhood and how it shaped you.

_____
_____
_____
_____
_____
_____
_____
_____
_____
_____
_____
_____
_____
_____
_____
_____

Appreciate all the stages that helps you blossom into the person you desire to be.

Step 2 - Acceptance

Accept your trauma. Accept that there is work to be done and take steps necessary to tend to your inner child.

Here are some affirmations that the wounded inner child needs to hear. You can practice saying them daily in front of a mirror, or say them to yourself in your quiet time:

- *I see you*
- *I love you*
- *I hear you*
- *I forgive you*
- *I understand*
- *You are enough*
- *You did your best*
- *I am proud of you*
- *You didn't deserve that*
- *Your opinion matters*

Write down 3 affirmations that your wounded inner child needs to hear, then say them aloud.

_____
_____
_____
_____
_____
_____
_____
_____
_____

Step 3 - Apologize & Release The Hurt

Write an apology letter to your inner child. Express yourself in the most vulnerable way. Apologize for the experiences you could not control and the ones you did not know would eventually control your life. Upon completion, release the emotions that you've been holding in. You can release through meditation, crying, yelling, or any way you feel compelled to.

To My Younger Self,

_____
_____
_____
_____
_____
_____
_____
_____
_____
_____
_____
_____
_____
_____
_____
_____
_____
_____
_____
_____
_____
_____
_____

Step 4: Reparent

Now it's time to reparent your inner child and create the life you needed. This will help you heal your wounds and be able to form healthy relationships in your life. It will help you redefine what love and life should look like then help you move on.

Reparenting your inner child can look like this:

- Going to therapy
- Creating new memories
- Recreating your memories
- Setting boundaries in all relationships
- Being the person your inner child needed
- Creating a safe and freeing space for yourself
- Replacing dysfunction family dynamics with healthy ones

Affirm:
I am creating a life worth living.

What is your inner child in need of?

1._____
_____

2._____
_____

3._____
_____

Describe your parents or guardian in 3 words.

1._____

2._____

3._____

Unhealthy family dynamics:

- Normalizing toxicity
- Being controlled
- Lack of boundaries
- Enduring abuse
- Poor Communication
- Being loved with conditions
- Dealing with narcissistic parents
- Children being "Seen & not heard"
- Lack of intimacy

Healthy family dynamics:

- Apologizing when necessary
- Allowing the space for everyone to develop their own morals, values, and desires
- Safe spaces and boundaries in place.
- Receiving support and guidance.
- Having the opportunity to voice your opinions.
- Experiencing unconditional love
- Allowing the space for children to feel and express their emotions.

Was your family dynamic healthy or unhealthy? What kinds of dynamics could you find in your family?

_____
_____
_____
_____
_____
_____
_____
_____
_____
_____
_____
_____

Write a letter to your mom or mother figure. *(If you did not have a mother figure in your life, write a letter about how this has affected you).*

Write a letter to your dad or father figure. *(If you did not have a father figure in your life, write a letter about how this has affected you).*

How do you feel about parenting? Do you want to become a parent?

_____
_____
_____
_____
_____

If you answered yes to becoming a parent, what are you looking forward to?

_____
_____
_____
_____
_____

If you answered no to becoming a parent, why don't you want to embark on that journey?

_____
_____
_____
_____
_____

What makes someone a good parent?

What are some fundamental beliefs or life skills you believe all children should be taught?

What are some of your favorite childhood memories? What memories would you like to recreate?

What is something you wish your parents provided for you or instilled in you? Why? *(Example: I wish my parents provided more support when growing up because the lack thereof turned me into a codependent person).*

_____
_____
_____
_____
_____
_____
_____

_____
_____
_____
_____
_____
_____
_____
_____
_____
_____
_____
_____
_____
_____
_____

What is something you wish your parents did not provide or instill in you? Why?
(Example: I wish my parents didn't teach me to always say yes or made me feel guilty when I said no, I am now a people-pleaser and I put others before myself).

___

**Forgive your parents for not being able to
love you the way you needed to be loved.**

As a child I wanted to be...

_____
_____
_____
_____
_____
_____
_____

Spending time with children makes me feel...

_____
_____
_____
_____
_____
_____
_____
_____
_____
_____
_____
_____
_____
_____
_____
_____

Write a letter giving your younger self advice.

Things To Keep In Mind

You are not subjected to live the life your family wants for you.

You are not required to keep unhealthy family dynamics in your life.

You can acknowledge and heal your inner child without blaming or confronting your parents for what it has done to you.

Say This Aloud:

My healing is my responsibility
My happiness is my responsibility
My success is my responsibility
My reaction is my responsibility
My life is my responsibility

Lessons and Thoughts

What are your takeaways from this chapter? What did you learn? What are your thoughts? Express it below.

_____
_____
_____
_____
_____
_____
_____
_____
_____
_____
_____
_____
_____
_____
_____
_____
_____
_____
_____
_____
_____
_____

Checking In...

How are you feeling today? Is anything weighing on your heart? Release it below in the form of a prayer, poem or simply writing it out the way it flows in your mind.

CHAPTER 3
When You've Hit Rock Bottom

Here's the thing about hitting rock bottom, the only place left to go is up. Hitting rock bottom can transform your life for the better if you allow it to. This is a time when you are forced to reflect on your life, what lead you to this point and whether you will be giving up or changing your life for the better.

It's never too late to start over.

Describe a time in your life where you believe you hit rock bottom.

_____
_____
_____
_____
_____
_____
_____
_____
_____
_____

How did you get through that time? Or how do you plan to?

Depression & Anxiety

Depression and anxiety are two of the most common mental disorders. Both disorders are unique to the person and can be very hard to detect. Depression is typically rooted in guilt, shame, abandonment, and other past traumas. Depression ranges from mild to severe. You may know someone who is life of the party. They may go to every event, motivate everyone else and can light up a room whenever they smile… but this same person may be broken inside. This person may struggle waking up each day because they never wanted to wake up to face another day. They may contemplate ending their life daily. Despite that feeling, somehow they manage to make someone else smile.

Depression can also look the opposite. Someone may say no to hanging out. They may fail classes. They may overeat or stop eating all together. They may be aggressive towards everyone who comes into their space or thoughts. It's an internal feeling that may or may not appear externally.

Many people reach the point of suicide because they did not address the root of their depression and found ways to cope. Whatever it is that is causing this feeling needs to be addressed. It's okay to not be okay but it's not okay to stay there.

Ways you can cope with depression:

- Reprograming your mind
- Going to a therapist
- Focusing on where you want to be and not where you are
- Remembering your why
- Practicing self-care
- Looking ahead – Stop looking at your past. Make peace with your past so you can move on. You cannot drive a car looking in the rear-view mirror.

- Redefining your life – The same way people rebrand a business, you can rebrand your life.
- Stepping back from what's causing you pain
- Doing random acts of kindness – volunteering, taking yourself out, etc.
- Getting sunlight & fresh air regularly
- Expressing gratitude for what you have, don't have and what's yet to come.
- Getting a substantial amount of sleep
- Partaking in activities that you enjoy even if you may not feel up for it
- Creating healthy routines

Sometimes all you have to do is show up. Show up for yourself each day. Put in a little bit of work each day and it will pay off. I need you to know that there is purpose in your pain, and you deserve a happy ending. Don't give up on yourself, keep going.

Have you ever been depressed? *Circle one.*

YES   NO

If yes, describe what depression looked like for you and what got you to that point.

_____
_____
_____
_____
_____
_____
_____
_____

Do you ever experience random waves of sadness? Nothing particularly happened but all of a sudden you have no energy to do anything. No hope for better days. No urge to keep going. No urge to smile. Unable to see the beauty in anything, Maybe you just want to curl up and cry.

How do you get through these times? What do you believe gets you to these moments?

_____
_____
_____
_____
_____
_____
_____
_____
_____
_____
_____
_____
_____
_____
_____
_____
_____
_____
_____
_____

No matter how major or minor your situation may feel, feel those emotions. Never neglect them. That's the only way you'll get through it.

Anxiety is typically caused by stress, fear and sudden stumbling blocks. Fear is a roadblock for so many people. The best way to combat fear when it concerns moving forward is to stop comparing yourself to others. **Your journey is unique to YOU.** You will go through things necessary to make you the person you need to be. The only time you need to look at others is for inspiration or collaboration!

Another thing that causes anxiety is thinking ahead or dwelling on the past. Instead of thinking ahead or dwelling on the past, aim to be present. Stop, breathe, and truly enjoy this moment. Yes, you can and must plan ahead to help you get the life you desire but don't get caught up living in/for the future or living in /for the past, that your life passes you by.

Things To Keep In Mind

Are your thoughts rational or irrational thoughts? Are your thoughts based on facts or feelings?

Feeling like a failure does not make you a failure. Failing at one thing does not mean you will fail at everything. Feeling like you are unloved does not mean you are unloved and it doesn't mean you don't deserve love.

Remember to focus on facts. Yes, feelings will always be involved. We are taught to follow our heart but that's not all there is to it.

I had to learn to focus on facts because my feelings had me feeling like the world was against me which is never the case. Focusing on facts will help you in many areas of life. Especially those who overthink like myself.

Are you experiencing anxiety about any area of your life now? *If yes, what about?*

_____
_____
_____
_____
_____
_____

Describe what anxiety looks and feels like for you.

_____
_____
_____
_____
_____
_____

Here is a grounding technique that is effective during times of anxiety. This simple activity can be used to bring you back to the current moment when you feel yourself getting increasingly anxious.

Identify:

5 Things you can see
4 Things you can touch
3 Things you can hear
2Things you can hear
1 Thing you can taste

Have you ever been suicidal? Circle One

YES   NO

If yes, describe what you think triggered those thoughts and desires.

_____
_____
_____
_____
_____
_____
_____
_____
_____
_____
_____
_____
_____
_____
_____
_____
_____
_____
_____
_____
_____
_____
_____
_____

"BREATHE, LET GO, AND REMEMBER THIS VERY MOMENT IS THE ONLY ONE YOU KNOW YOU HAVE FOR SURE."
OPRAH WINFREY

What steps can you take to make your life more livable and prevent suicidal thoughts in the future?

What are your takeaways from this chapter? What did you learn? What are your thoughts? Express it below.

Checking In...

How are you feeling today? Is anything weighing on your heart? Release it below in the form of a prayer, poem or simply writing it out the way it flows in your mind.

_____
_____
_____
_____
_____
_____
_____
_____
_____
_____
_____
_____
_____
_____
_____
_____
_____
_____
_____
_____
_____
_____
_____

CHAPTER 4
Forgiveness

What is the first thing that comes to mind when you hear the word *forgiveness*?

_____
_____
_____
_____
_____
_____
_____
_____
_____

"True forgiveness is when you can say, 'Thank you for that experience.'"
-Oprah Winfrey

Are you carrying around unforgiveness, anger, guilt, resentment, secrets, or shame from your childhood? If yes, what are the burdens you are carrying and why are you struggling to let them go?

Forgiving Someone

Forgiveness is one of the most important steps of the healing process. A common misconception of forgiveness is that you must wait till the offender apologizes. Forgiveness does not require an apology. It does not need to be done in a specific amount of time and most importantly, forgiveness is not for the offender's benefit. You forgive someone for yourself.

Once you've forgiven your offender, you allow yourself to release the pain and be at peace. When you refuse to forgive someone, you choose to harbor pain and resentment which will drain your energy and cause you more pain in the future.

Forgiving Yourself

Forgiving yourself is just as substantial as forgiving others. Without forgiveness, you will carry around guilt and shame. You will continue to relive that moment and may hurt another person in the exact same way. When you harbor guilt and shame, you may start to believe that this is who you are. You may think you are a bad person and you're unchangeable which is what could lead to you hurting another person the same way.

Steps to forgiving yourself:

1. Take time to process what happened
2. Acknowledge where things went wrong
3. Take responsibility for your actions
4. Apologize to the victim
5. Accept whatever consequences, if any
6. Learn from this mistake
7. Let go of your guilt & shame
8. Leave your past in the past & allow yourself to be at peace

Who do you have resentment towards?

Why are you harboring resentment towards these person (s)?

"If you are still breathing, you have your second chance."
Oprah Winfrey

What is something you need to forgive yourself for?

Do you allow yourself to make mistakes and learn from them?

Think about that old friend, family member, or ex who still lives in your mind due to your harbored pain and resentment towards them. Write a goodbye letter to this person and release any pain associated with them. Allow yourself to achieve inner peace by forgiving them and moving forward.

Lessons and Thoughts

What are your takeaways from this chapter? What did you learn? What are your thoughts? Express it below.

_____
_____
_____
_____
_____
_____
_____
_____
_____
_____
_____
_____
_____
_____
_____
_____
_____
_____
_____
_____
_____
_____
_____
_____
_____

Checking In...

How are you feeling today? Is anything weighing on your heart? Release it below in the form of a prayer, poem or simply writing it out the way it flows in your mind.

_____
_____
_____
_____
_____
_____
_____
_____
_____
_____
_____
_____
_____
_____
_____
_____
_____
_____
_____
_____
_____
_____
_____
_____
_____

Create The Life You Want

"Success is not the key to happiness.
Happiness is the key to success.
If you love what you are doing, you will be successful."

CHAPTER 5
Reprogramming Our Mind

The mind has 3 levels. The conscious, subconscious, the unconscious mind.

The conscious mind is what we use to analyze, plan, and make decisions with. It involves all the things we are aware of.

Our subconscious mind is where you find the information just below awareness. It stores and retrieves our memories and experiences which we use to determine our beliefs and values. This state of mind is what guides you.

When the day has come to an end, the unconscious mind gets to work. This is the creator and storage unit for our dreams. The unconscious mind also sorts through all the information gathered throughout the day. Important and unimportant things will get passed to their appropriate file in the mind. The unconscious mind also remembers the things we absolutely can't forget (for example, breathing.)

Here's an analogy to help you understand each category of the mind:

Let's say you've moved to a new city, and you are driving to your new job for the first time. You may use a GPS or a physical map to help you with your directions. You will pay attention to the street names and what turns you must make. You will pay attention to the roads you're on and how long it will take. This is all done with your conscious mind. Being present and analyzing your route.

As you learn this route and get into a routine, you'll no longer have to use your GPS. You'll know what time you need to leave the house to be on time. You'll know every turn you have to make without looking at which street you're on. All these instructions are stored in your subconscious mind and forms this habit/routine. If you happen to be late, you'll then use your conscious mind to analyze possibly taking another route to beat traffic, etc.

The music the cars around you were playing are not important in your routine. The colors of the cars around you are not important for your routine. This unimportant information gets pushed to unconscious mind. Even though it's in the unconscious mind, you still can recall and reflect on it but it is not substantial enough to linger in your subconscious or conscious mind.

A habit is when the body knows how to do it better than the mind. Meaning, you won't think about it, you'll just do it.

Your subconscious mind is the most important state of mind. The conscious mind only takes up 5% of your minds function. Even though this is the state of mind that we use to make every decision, all our thoughts, reactions, feelings, and experiences we'll use when analyzing/deciding comes from what is stored in the subconscious mind. Everything you see, hear and have done will sit here until it has a reason to step into your conscious mind.

So, my question to you is: What is your subconscious mind filled with?

What comes natural to you? Is it thoughts and actions that will lead you to success and happiness?

Or is it negative or shallow routines to keep you stagnant in life? In what ways have you been conditioned?

Release what's in your subconscious mind. This is the first step to reprogramming your mind.

Meditating is a great way to help you get control of your mind. Meditation is about being still, and learning how to let go of the thoughts. Focus on this current moment. Fight the urge to get up. Fight the urge to react. This will help you think before you speak. This will help you listen to understand instead of listening to respond. Meditating can really help you become the best version of yourself.

Do you meditate? If yes, how has this impacted your life. If no, how can it help your life?

"If you can't change it, change the way you think about it."
Maya Angelou

Quazi Johir teaches an interesting concept that aids with reprogramming the mind. It focuses on the external (incoming) and internal (outgoing) thoughts we have and how we react to them. Based on our emotion towards these thoughts, it can form belief. Once you start to believe it, our RAS (Reticular Activating System) gets programmed or conditioned. These conditions get stored in the subconscious mind. Once you've been conditioned to believe this, you start to look for confirmation of it. What you look for, you will find. The more you confirm this thought, it will lead to a conviction.

Incoming (External) thoughts are the thoughts and opinions that gets projected onto us. This can be from someone telling you that you won't be successful. Or a show you're watching that displays a lot of negativity. Although it's been projected, you do not have to accept it. Once accepted, it becomes an Outgoing (Internal) thought.

Outgoing (Internal) thoughts are the ones you choose for yourself. Even if someone is telling you that you won't be successful, you do not have to accept it. You can leave that negative comment in the comment section! If you don't accept it, it won't become an outgoing (internal) thought and it will not be able to condition you.

The emotion you have towards this thought will determine whether or not you accept it or start to believe it. Understand that everyone will have opinions. Everyone will look at life differently. You must cling to what brings you joy and peace. If their opinions won't lead to elevation or joy, leave it where it is! When you believe the thoughts being projected on to you, you give that person power that they don't deserve. People will try to tear you down every step of the way but it's on you to decide what you do with it. No one knows your future but you and God! God is making the way and you are making it happen.

Our RAS (Reticular Activating System) is responsible for our ability to focus, our fight or flight response, how we perceive the world, and most importantly being a gatekeeper for information we need to focus on. This controls and connects what's in the subconscious mind into consciousness.

When the RAS is programmed or conditioned to believe something, we will seek out confirmation of it. For instance, if your RAS is programmed to focus on your success, the bright side and growth, you will be unaffected by negativity thrown at you.

For example, if you're reading reviews of your product, you will only focus on the positivity to confirm the manifestations you have for yourself. This does not mean you won't acknowledge negative reviews. It means it will all be surface level for you. You will take the opinions as they are, opinions. You'll take the constructive criticism apply what needs to be applied for your elevation. And most of all you will acknowledge and celebrate yourself when reading the good reviews as well.

If someone's RAS is programmed with shame and doubt, this person will not notice the positive reviews. They will only focus on the negative reviews. Whether it's by beating themselves up about it or trying to bash the person who left the review. However, it's done, this person will walk away with the same shame and doubt they walked in with because they have just received a confirmation of it.

Once you have been programmed and seek confirmations of these programs, you will become convicted. You will believe this is what life should look like for you and it will be so hard to tell you otherwise or change this mindset of yours. You should strive to be convicted of a life where you know you deserve peace, success, and happiness.

Have you ever interacted with someone who is always happy? Like no matter what, this person always has something positive to say. For most people, that seems weird. But this is what we all should be striving for. Life will always do what life does. But how we face the world is based on how we've been conditioned to see the world.

THOUGHTS ARE THE
VOCABULARY OF THE BRAIN.

FEELINGS ARE THE
VOCABULARY OF THE BODY.

What conviction do you want to receive? How do you want to program your mind?

"Watch your thoughts, they become your words; watch your words, they become your actions; watch your actions, they become your habits; watch your habits, they become your character; watch your character, it becomes your destiny."

What kind of thoughts/opinions do people have of you?

For example, *"Why are you starting a business that you know will fail?"*

_____
_____
_____
_____
_____
_____
_____
_____
_____
_____

Do you believe them? Are you accepting them? If yes, replace them below with the opposite that will you bring you joy!

For example, *"My business will be very successful because I will put in the work to make sure of it!"*

_____
_____
_____
_____
_____
_____
_____
_____
_____
_____

In what ways can you confirm these thoughts?

For example, you can confirm/reassure your business is becoming successful by celebrating after investing in your inventory or finishing your website.

"You don't need to be great to get started but you need to get started to be great."
Les Brown

Does your environment control your thinking or does your thinking control your environment? How?

If we become who we say we are. Who are you?

"If you listen to any thought long enough, it will become a part of your personal playlist."
- *Jon Acuff*

"Still I Rise"
BY MAYA ANGELOU

You may write me down in history
With your bitter, twisted lies,
You may tread me in the very dirt
But still, like dust, I'll rise.
Does my sassiness upset you?
Why are you beset with gloom?
'Cause I walk like I've got oil wells
Pumping in my living room.
Just like moons and like suns,
With the certainty of tides,
Just like hopes springing high,
Still I'll rise.
Did you want to see me broken?
Bowed head and lowered eyes?
Shoulders falling down like teardrops.
Weakened by my soulful cries.
Does my haughtiness offend you?
Don't you take it awful hard
'Cause I laugh like I've got gold mines
Diggin' in my own back yard.
You may shoot me with your words,
You may cut me with your eyes,
You may kill me with your hatefulness,
But still, like air, I'll rise.
Does my sexiness upset you?
Does it come as a surprise
That I dance like I've got diamonds
At the meeting of my thighs?
Out of the huts of history's shame
I rise
Up from a past that's rooted in pain
I rise
I'm a black ocean, leaping and wide,
Welling and swelling I bear in the tide.
Leaving behind nights of terror and fear
I rise
Into a daybreak that's wondrously clear
I rise
Bringing the gifts that my ancestors gave,
I am the dream and the hope of the slave.
I rise
I rise
I rise.

What were your take aways from this poem?

Lessons and Thoughts

What are your takeaways from this chapter? What did you learn? What are your thoughts? Express it below.

_____
_____
_____
_____
_____
_____
_____
_____
_____
_____
_____
_____
_____
_____
_____
_____
_____
_____
_____
_____
_____

Checking In...

How are you feeling today? Is anything weighing on your heart? Release it below in the form of a prayer, poem or simply writing it out the way it flows in your mind.

_____
_____
_____
_____
_____
_____
_____
_____
_____
_____
_____
_____
_____
_____
_____
_____
_____
_____
_____
_____
_____
_____
_____
_____
_____

CHAPTER 6

What is the first thing that comes to your mind when you hear the word *manifestation*?

_____
_____
_____
_____
_____
_____
_____
_____
_____

What worries you the most about your future?

_____
_____
_____
_____
_____
_____
_____
_____
_____

Manifestation is the transmutation of thoughts into your physical reality. In simpler words, this means speaking things into existence. Regardless of your ethnicity, religious or non-religious beliefs, manifestation can be used to enhance the life you have or create the life you desire.

By believing you can achieve something, you are setting yourself up for success. Although manifestation is the utilization of words, your actions must still reflect the outcome you desire. You must still take the necessary steps required.

I like to think of a manifestation as the brain and the body not fully synced. Once I've manifested the goal I want to achieve, I just need to give my body/physical reality a chance to catch up.

Create some manifestations below.

By this time next year, I will be…

_____
_____
_____
_____
_____
_____
_____
_____
_____
_____
_____
_____
_____

In the next five years I will be...

_____
_____
_____
_____
_____
_____
_____
_____
_____
_____

In the next 6 months, my body will be...

_____
_____
_____
_____
_____
_____
_____
_____
_____
_____

My future will be...

"You don't become what you want, you become what you believe"
Oprah Winfrey

What are your takeaways from this chapter? What did you learn? What are your thoughts? Express it below.

Checking In...

How are you feeling today? Is anything weighing on your heart? Release it below in the form of a prayer, poem or simply writing it out the way it flows in your mind.

_____
_____
_____
_____
_____
_____
_____
_____
_____
_____
_____
_____
_____
_____
_____
_____
_____
_____
_____
_____
_____
_____
_____
_____

CHAPTER 7
Goals

Goal setting is a great way to plan out the life you desire. Your
 will give you a sense of direction and structure, while providing you with motivation to make it to the finish line. Goal setting also holds you accountable to yourself.

Tips for setting goals:

- Discipline
- Be committed to your commitment
- Be specific with each goal
    - ✓ The more specific the goal, the easier it will be to focus on it and take the necessary steps toward it. For example, if you have a goal to own your home, figure out smaller details about the home you desire, such as its location, size, amenities, price and so on.
- Create goals that are realistic for YOU
    - ✓ Goals realistic for your friends or role models may not be realistic for you. Select goals realistic for your age, skillset, personality, resources and other circumstances
- Give each goal a deadline
    - ✓ When a goal has no deadline, it often gets pushed to the side.
- Create both long term and short-term goals.
    - ✓ Having a short-term goal as a first stop prior to your long-term goal will help create a smoother process and may make you achieve the long-term goal faster.
- Make a plan with steps necessary to achieve each goal
- Set up periodical reviews at set times such as quarterly, to check your progress and adjust the plan for each goal as necessary.

One day or Day one. You decide.

Are you actively setting goals in your life? *(Circle one).*

YES   NO

What can you do to improve your goal setting habits?

_____
_____
_____
_____
_____
_____
_____
_____
_____
_____
_____
_____
_____
_____
_____
_____
_____
_____
_____
_____
_____

Do what's hard while it's easy.

What are your mental health goals?

_____
_____
_____
_____
_____
_____
_____
_____
_____
_____
_____
_____

What is required to achieve these goals?

_____
_____
_____
_____
_____
_____
_____
_____
_____
_____
_____
_____

How will your life look once you've achieved your mental health goals?

Affirm:
I will remain focused on my goal.
I am achieving all my goals.
I am blossoming into the person I desire to be.

What are your physical health goals?

_____
_____
_____
_____
_____
_____
_____
_____
_____
_____
_____
_____
_____
_____

What is required to achieve these goals?

_____
_____
_____
_____
_____
_____
_____
_____
_____
_____
_____
_____
_____
_____

How will your life look once you've achieved your physical health goals?

Affirm:
I will remain focused on my goal.
I am achieving all my goals.
I am blossoming into the person I desire to be.

What are your financial health goals?

_____
_____
_____
_____
_____
_____
_____
_____
_____
_____
_____
_____

What is required to achieve these goals?

_____
_____
_____
_____
_____
_____
_____
_____
_____
_____
_____
_____

How will your life look once you've achieved your financial health goals?

Affirm:
I will remain focused on my goal.
I am achieving all my goals.
I am blossoming into the person I desire to be.

Remove "*But*" from your vocabulary and replace it with "*So.*"

Example:
I want to go back to school but I know I can't handle it.
I want to go back to school so I'm going to start looking at school options.

What creates a "But" in your life? Write that sentence then rewrite it with so.

_____
_____
_____
_____
_____
_____
_____
_____
_____
_____
_____
_____
_____
_____
_____
_____
_____

*"What you get by achieving your goals is not as important as
who you become while achieving your goals."*
Henry Thoreau

What has been your greatest accomplishment so far in life?

Affirm:
I am creating a life that I will not need an escape from.

Create a bucket list.

In what ways have you changed this month?

Your only competition is yourself.
Aim to be better than the person you were yesterday.

What weaknesses can you turn into strengths?

_____
_____
_____
_____
_____
_____
_____
_____
_____

How do you react to failure?

_____
_____
_____
_____
_____
_____
_____
_____
_____

"If you can imagine it, you can achieve it.
If you can dream it, you can become it."
William Arthur

What are your takeaways from this chapter? What did you learn? What are your thoughts? Express it below.

_____
_____
_____
_____
_____
_____
_____
_____
_____
_____
_____
_____
_____
_____
_____
_____
_____
_____
_____
_____

Checking In...

How are you feeling today? Is anything weighing on your heart? Release it below in the form of a prayer, poem or simply writing it out the way it flows in your mind.

CHAPTER 8
Building Healthy Relationships

Your attachment style is what determines or explains the way you interact and behave in relationships.

Attachment Styles

1. **Secure**

If your attachment style is secure, you are not avoidant or anxious about being attached to others. This means you are comfortable with forming secure and loving relationships. You are trusting with others and open to being intimate. You do not fear rejection or distance in your relationships. You want to experience strong bonds and meaningful connections.

2. **Avoidant**

If your attachment style is avoidant, you have a high level of avoidance but low anxiety level. This means you have trouble connecting with others. You get anxious about opening up. You generally come across as emotionally distant due to you having a wall up. You have trust issues, and you give your partner and friends plenty of space to avoid getting too close.

3. **Anxious**

If your attachment style is anxious, you have low levels of avoidance but high levels of anxiety towards being attached to others. This means you are very insecure in your relationships. You are often referred to as clingy due to your fear of abandonment. You crave intimacy, validation and quality time all the time.

4. Fearful Avoidant

If your attachment style is Fearful Avoidant, you have high levels of avoidance and anxiety. This means you are hard to analyze in your relationships. You send many mixed signals by seeking attention one moment and avoiding it the next moment. You fear getting too close or too attached to your partner. Love and commitment are very scary concepts for you.

What is your attachment style?

_____
_____

How has your attachment style impacted your relationships?

_____
_____
_____
_____
_____
_____
_____
_____
_____
_____
_____
_____
_____
_____
_____

In what ways do you potentially push people away?

Who or what comes to mind when you hear the word *toxic*?

A toxic relationship is a relationship between two people that causes a strain on someone's mental, physical or financial health. These relationships can make one or both partners feel trapped, unloved and worthless.

Toxic Traits & Red Flags to look out for:
- Lack of support
- Jealousy
- Gaslighting
- Abuse of any kind
- Manipulation
- Control
- Lack of respect

If you deal with any or all of these, I urge you to seek professional guidance on next steps towards improving your emotional health and the future of your relationship. Dealing with these character traits are likely to deplete your self-esteem and lead to depression. It is very hard to recover from a toxic relationship once it hits rock bottom. Many people are unfortunately accustomed and desensitized to toxicity. They may have had a toxic family, which predisposed them to be accepting of toxic friends or toxic partners.

To an individual who's never experienced a truly healthy relationship, toxic relationships may be viewed as healthy. A true healthy relationship will be unfamiliar to them. In most cases, such a person will reject a chance to have a healthy relationship until they have healed and learned what a healthy relationship should genuinely look and feel like.

Are you attracting toxic relationships? Circle one.

YES   NO

Have you ever been the toxic person in a relationship? If so, in what ways were you toxic?

_____
_____
_____
_____
_____
_____
_____
_____
_____
_____
_____
_____
_____
_____
_____
_____
_____
_____
_____
_____

Have you ever been in a relationship with a toxic person? If yes, who was the toxic person? In what ways were they toxic? How did it affect you?

Do you have healthy relationships in your life? If so, what makes you describe them as healthy relationships?

_____
_____
_____
_____
_____
_____
_____
_____
_____
_____
_____

How do you feel when your friends and family achieve something?

_____
_____
_____
_____
_____
_____
_____
_____
_____
_____
_____

Are you an introvert or extrovert?

___

How are you impacting the people in your life?

___

Do your loved ones celebrate your successes? How so?

Unlearning Myths About Love:

You can love someone and get angry with them.
You can love someone and still be disappointed in them.
You can love someone while working on yourself.
You can love someone and still walk away from the relationship.

Do you set healthy boundaries in your relationships?

_____
_____
_____
_____
_____
_____
_____
_____
_____
_____

What boundaries do you need to set or reinforce in your relationships?

_____
_____
_____
_____
_____
_____
_____
_____
_____
_____
_____
_____

Write a letter of appreciation to someone in your life who genuinely loves and supports you. I encourage you to share this letter with the person.

Who is someone that you are not related to by blood, but consider family? Why?

Individuality

Many couples fuse into one person as they get deeper into their relationship. They start to read the same books, listen to the same songs, do every activity together, go everywhere together and even adopt each other's opinions. Doing a few or most things together in your relationship is great. Doing everything together will create a problem as your individuality will decrease.

The lack of individuality in relationships can cause one or both partners to feel suffocated. Too much of anything is never good and this applies here. Embracing your individuality will create personal happiness and further contribute to your relationships. It will give you a sense of self-worth and give you something that you can call your own.

Maintaining individuality in your relationships is vital. Who are you outside of your partner? Regardless of whether you have been married or committed for 5 or even 10 years, you need to be your own individual. You need to trust yourself, love yourself and be there for yourself.

Ways You Can Maintain Individuality In Your Relationship
- Spend time alone
- Engage in some activities without your partner present
- Pursue your personal goals
- Avoid becoming co-dependent
- Give your partner space to blossom and grow
- Maintain the interests you had prior to the relationship

How are you maintaining individuality in your relationships? If you are not doing so, how will you start to do this?

_____
_____
_____
_____
_____
_____
_____
_____
_____
_____
_____
_____

Have you ever burned a bridge in a relationship that you wish you could rebuild?

_____
_____
_____
_____
_____
_____
_____
_____
_____
_____
_____
_____

What qualities do you look for in a friend?

Are you giving what you want to receive from your friends?

Describe the best relationship that you've ever been in. What made this relationship so great to you? (This can be platonic or romantic.)

_____
_____
_____
_____
_____
_____
_____
_____
_____
_____
_____
_____
_____

How would your family describe you?

_____
_____
_____
_____
_____
_____
_____
_____
_____
_____
_____
_____
_____

How would your friends describe you?

How do you want people to describe you?

Name something you absolutely won't compromise on.

_____
_____
_____
_____
_____
_____
_____
_____
_____
_____

Which relationship have you recently outgrown? Why did it no longer serve you?

_____
_____
_____
_____
_____
_____
_____
_____
_____
_____
_____

Affirm:

Everything that I need, I already have.

Everything that I have is all that I need.

Everything I desire will be received.

Because my reality is created by me.

Love

Affirm:
I will lead with love.
I am deserving of love.
I am surrounded by love.
I attract loving relationships.
I am loving to those around me.
I will love myself unconditionally.
I will allow myself to be loved unconditionally.

What is the first thing that comes to mind when you hear the word *love*?

_____
_____
_____
_____
_____
_____
_____
_____
_____
_____
_____
_____

1. Physical Touch
You feel most loved when you are physically embraced. This can be by hugging, kissing, holding hands, massages, cuddling, etc. Intimacy is a priority in all relationships for you. You are extremely affectionate with friends, family, and romantic partners.

2. Acts of Service
You feel most loved when someone does something for you or helps you complete a task and lightens your load. This can be someone making dinner, doing your laundry, or washing your car. People with this love language do not feel loved if someone sits or stands by and watch, rather than giving you a helping hand.

3. Quality Time
You feel most loved when someone spends quality time with you. This can be done virtually or in person. You enjoy going on dates, hanging out or just anything that involves you and that person being engaged in each other's company. You value active listening and getting undivided attention. This means that simply being together is not enough if the person is on their phone, watching television or multitasking in any other way.

4. Receiving Gifts
You feel most loved when you receive gifts. These gifts do not have to be a specific type, price range, or holiday based. People with this love language enjoys receiving random tokens such as money for lunch, flowers, or a new pair of shoes.

5. Words of Affirmation
You feel most loved when you are affirmed verbally. Regardless of what someone may do, you wait till their thoughts or feelings are put into words. You enjoying hearing or reading phrases such as *"I love you"; "You look beautiful"* and *"We are in this together."*

Based on the information provided above, rank the 5 love language in order from which matters most to you, to which matters least to you. *If you are not sure, you can take* the *free test online* at www.5lovelanguages.com *to help you figure it out.*

1. _____

2. _____

3. _____

4. _____

5. _____

Do you know your loved ones' main love language? Circle one.

YES   NO

If yes, are you catering to their love language? Circle one.

YES   NO

If no, list the names of 3 of your loved ones. Think about what you have done in the past that has pleased them, and write what you believe their main love language is.

_____
_____
_____
_____
_____
_____
_____
_____
_____
_____
_____
_____
_____
_____
_____
_____
_____

Write a love letter to yourself.

Do you want to find love? Why or why not?

What do you think it means to love someone from a distance?

If loving someone is causing you pain mentally, physically or financially, you may need to consider loving this person from a distance. Loving someone from a distance can look like:

- Moving out if you live together
- Limiting interaction by reducing how often you have conversations, and the length of those conversations
- Ending a relationship
- Reducing face-to-face interactions
- Returning any borrowed possessions

Loving someone from a distance does not mean you need to cut them out of your life completely. For some people, that may be the best choice but for many others, this just gives the relationship the space and boundaries necessary for growth. It may also be what you need to enhance your mental health.

Love does not require you to stick around. It does not require communication or any obligations. Above all, you must love yourself first and love yourself enough to step back if anything becomes damaging for your mental, physical or financial health.

If prioritizing your needs and protecting your peace is selfish, then so be it.

Is there anyone that you need to start loving from a distance? If so, why?

Don't lose yourself trying to save someone.

Is loving someone scary for you? Why or why not?

What does unconditional love look/feel like for you?

Write a love letter to your current or future partner.

CHAPTER 9
Health: Mental, Physical & Financial

Mental Health

Have you ever been to a therapy session? If so, what was your experience? If not, why not?

_____
_____
_____
_____
_____
_____
_____

What is something that drains your energy?

_____
_____
_____
_____
_____
_____
_____

How you feel mentally can transcribe physically.

In what ways do you need to put yourself before others?

_____
_____
_____
_____
_____
_____
_____
_____
_____
_____

What matters most in your life?

_____
_____
_____
_____
_____
_____
_____
_____
_____
_____

Why do you matter?

_____
_____
_____
_____
_____
_____
_____
_____
_____
_____

Do you have a safe space? Circle one.

YES   NO

What does a safe space look like for you?

_____
_____
_____
_____
_____
_____
_____
_____

Do you seek approval from others? Circle one.

YES NO

What wounds do you need to heal?

_____
_____
_____
_____
_____
_____
_____
_____
_____
_____
_____
_____
_____
_____
_____
_____
_____
_____
_____
_____

Affirm:
Heal until you can trust again.
Heal until you can love again.
Heal until you feel whole again.
And after all that healing, there's still room to heal some more.

If you could live a life free of judgement, filled with support and like-minded individuals, what would your life look like?

Affirm:
I am unlearning the things that no longer contributes to my mental health

What is something you wish more people knew about you?

Describe a life-changing moment in your life.

If you could change one thing about yourself, what would it be?

Focus less on how far you have to go and more on how far you've come.

How does social media impact your life?

What is your biggest fear in life? Is this a rational or irrational fear?

Does your fear come from logic or trauma?

_____
_____
_____
_____
_____
_____
_____
_____
_____
_____

What can you do to keep this fear at bay?

_____
_____
_____
_____
_____
_____
_____
_____
_____
_____

Your fear of failure should never outweigh your desire to succeed.

As you're beginning to unlearn myths of life, use the space below to tell yourself *it's okay*.

I'll start you off
It's okay to say no.
It's okay to be indecisive
It's okay to walk away from relationships that no longer serve me
It's okay to have big dreams and aspirations for my self.

Keep it going...

What injustices impact you the most?

_____
_____
_____
_____
_____
_____
_____
_____
_____
_____
_____

What are some actions that you can take personally, at your job, in your community or country to contribute to progress in these areas?

_____
_____
_____
_____
_____
_____
_____
_____
_____
_____

What does happiness look like to you?

_____
_____
_____
_____
_____
_____
_____
_____
_____
_____

Do you have any regrets? If yes, what are they? *After you write them here, commit to leaving them on this page and accept how the situation turned out.*

_____
_____
_____
_____
_____
_____
_____
_____
_____
_____

Create 3 inspirational quotes for yourself.

1. _____
_____
_____

2. _____
_____
_____

3. _____
_____
_____

What needs to be removed from your life to help you be at peace?

_____
_____
_____
_____
_____
_____
_____
_____
_____
_____
_____
_____
_____

What role does music play in your life?

___

What are some habits and behaviors that you need to let go of? Commit to this change by completing the sentence below.

I will no longer feed into...

___

Look at yourself in the mirror for 6 minutes. Really look and stare. Twist, turn, shake and bend. Observe your body and all its parts. See yourself from head to toe.

Who/what did you see?

_____
_____
_____
_____
_____
_____
_____
_____
_____
_____
_____
_____

How did you feel?

_____
_____
_____
_____
_____
_____
_____
_____
_____

Describe a time in your life when you felt the most at peace and secure.

Physical Health

Do you like your body? Why or why not? If no, what can you do to change the way you feel about your body?

_____
_____
_____
_____
_____
_____
_____
_____
_____

If your body could speak, what would it say?

_____
_____
_____
_____
_____
_____
_____
_____
_____
_____
_____

What are you lacking in your physical diet?

Financial Health

Affirm:
I am a money magnet.
Money flows to me effortlessly.
My income exceeds my expenses.
My bills are paid.
My wants and needs are fulfilled.
I am rich in health.
I am rich in wealth.

What does financial freedom look like to you?

_____
_____
_____
_____
_____
_____
_____
_____
_____
_____
_____
_____

Tips to attain financial freedom
- Saving
- Paying off debt
- Monitoring your credit score
- Budgeting
- Attaining multiple streams of income

SAVING

Put money aside every time you receive money. Do this consistently and it will become easy to save. Make saving a priority in your financial diet! Treat your savings like a bill and it will become so easy to save. Don't be the person that pays their bills, spends leisure money then see whatever is left over to possibly save. Pay your bills then pay yourself by saving. Whatever is left can be used for leisure.

You can save for specific things or just a general rainy-day fund. Your savings will be the money you need to fall back on if you lose your income. Or what you need to secure your seat on the upcoming trip. Save for fun, emergencies, or peace of mind.

Make a list of things you need to save for with specific categories. Be as detailed as possible. How much you need? When's the deadline? What the expenses will cover specifically, etc.?

_____
_____
_____
_____
_____
_____
_____
_____
_____
_____
_____
_____
_____
_____
_____
_____
_____
_____
_____
_____

PAYING OFF DEBT

This includes all debt. Money you may owe a friend, family member or the bank. You can make small payments until you pay off your debt. America thrives on debt. Don't fall into that trap.

Make a list of any debt you owe and a date by which you wish to pay them off.

MONITORING YOUR CREDIT

Once you start becoming independent, you need to educate yourself on credit. Building substantial credit is important. It is a key that opens the door to new opportunities. Whether that's buying a house, getting a new car or a high credit limit on a credit card.

Credit factors - This is what the credit bureaus use to score you.

- **Payment history** - This makes up about 35% of your score. This is the most important factor in determining your credit score. Your payment history should be 100%. Any missed payments will hurt your score. This is not based on the balances paid in full. This is simply scored on whether you missed a payment or not. Being consistent with your lenders is extremely important to the creditor. It makes you look reliable and will help you with getting more loans in the future.

- **Revolving utilization** - This makes up about 30% of your credit score. This is used to track how much money you spend/how much money you owe. With credit cards, it's important to keep your utilization rate below 25%.

    For example: If you have a credit limit of $1000, try to keep your balance below $250. That is only 25% of use which looks great in the eyes of the lenders. As your credit score increases, your credit limits can increase which will gives you more room to spend. You can go above 25% but it's imperative to pay off the balance as soon as possible so it won't sit on your credit.

- **Credit history length** - This makes up about 15% of your credit score. This shows how long you've had open accounts on your credit.

    The length of credit is based on the average of all accounts. For example, if you got your first credit card 2 years ago and you got your last credit card today, your credit length will be 1 year. This is just the average of the oldest and the most recent items on your credit history. The longer your credit history is, the more reliable you"ll appear to lenders.

- **Amount of debt/total accounts**- This makes up about 10% of your score. You can manage a mix of loans without that hurting you. In the eyes of the creditor, the more accounts you have, the better it looks. As long as you keep the balances low and your credit will continue to grow.

- **Credit inquiries.**— This takes up about 10% of your credit score. This calculates the number of hard inquiries in the past year. Do not excessively apply for loans in a short period of time. Give your credit space and time to grow in between your applications.

    Examples of hard inquiries:
    Auto loans
    Mortgage loans
    Student loans
    Credit card applications

Were you aware of the credit factors?

YES   NO

What is your credit score?
You can get your score for free using Experian.com or provided by your banks. For instance, Chase, Capital 1. And discover all offer a free credit monitoring portal from your banking app or online banking site.

_____
_____

What can be done to improve your credit score?

BUDGETING

Budgeting is the key to financial freedom. Knowing when to spend and how much to spend will help you avoid debt, build credit, and help you save! Make a list of all your expenses and calculate how much you'll need bi weekly or monthly to make ends meet. Once your bills are paid, see what's left over for you. That's the money you can use to save, invest or use for leisure. It's vital to pay all your bills first, in full and on time.

Use the next few pages to create a budget

CREATE MULTIPLE STREAMS OF INCOME

Multiple streams of income will ensure you are set financially. You can have 9-5 while having businesses on the side. Or you can have multiple businesses that sell/cater to different people. There are so many ways to make money.

What passions can you turn into profit? How?

_____
_____
_____
_____
_____
_____
_____
_____
_____
_____

(Example) How To Turn Your Passion Into A Profit
Let's say you enjoy baking. Here's a list of different ways you can benefit financially.

- You can make bake goods to sell.
- You can create a class teaching people how to bake or decorate their baked goods.
- You can create a recipe book.
- You can become a YouTuber or any kind of public figure/influencer teaching, advertising, educating or entertaining people with baking content.
- You can create merchandise for bakers.

This ONE passion of yours has the opportunity to make you thousands of dollars...What are you waiting on?

If you won the lottery today, how would you utilize the money?

What are you lacking in your financial diet?

Lessons and Thoughts

What are your takeaways from this chapter? What did you learn? What are your thoughts? Express it below.

Checking In...

How are you feeling today? Is anything weighing on your heart? Release it below in the form of a prayer, poem or simply writing it out the way it flows in your mind.

_____
_____
_____
_____
_____
_____
_____
_____
_____
_____
_____
_____
_____
_____
_____
_____
_____
_____
_____
_____
_____
_____
_____
_____
_____

Maintaining The Gains

CHAPTER 10
Self-Love & Self Care

What does self-love mean to you? What does it look like for you?

_____
_____
_____
_____
_____
_____
_____
_____
_____
_____
_____
_____
_____
_____
_____
_____
_____
_____
_____
_____
_____

Unlearning the Myths about Self-Love

- You can love others while loving yourself
- You can wear makeup even though you love yourself
- You can alter your body even though you love yourself
- Self-love is not selfish
- You will still experience pain and sadness even though you love yourself
- The effects of self-love are not just temporary
- Self-love and self-care are not just for women

Self-love is the key to inner peace and happiness. It's the kind of love that makes you feel safe, seen, and confident. This love knows no bounds and has no conditions. This love helps you understand your value. This love lets you know your potential, your worth. You'll know that you deserve it all. You'll know that you are worthy of being loved.

It allows you to take the advice you give. It allows you to be okay when you don't fit in. Self-love is loving who you see in the mirror even on your worst days. You'll become your biggest inspiration. It's the love that removes fear and doubt. It's the love that always put you first. It's the love that pushes you to choose you, every time. You'll no longer seek validation.

Self-love is simply prioritizing yourself. Self-love is loving yourself the way you want to be loved. It includes allowing yourself to experience joy, success, growth and inner peace. It is about providing yourself with the support you want others to give you. It's about ensuring that you are protected even if everyone else fails to do so for you.

The love of self is vital. This love will give you the strength to make tough decisions to protect yourself. It will give you confidence and help you find your place in the world. Love is an action word. Although taking yourself out to eat or buying yourself new shoes is indeed a form of self-love, The mental aspect of it is far more important than the materialistic aspect. Self-love will look differently for everyone because it will be based on your love language.

Jen Oliver profoundly said, *"If you love the life you live, you'll have the life you love."* **What does this mean to you?**

Food For Thought:

How can you love someone if you don't love yourself?

How do you expect someone to love you if you don't love yourself?

You show someone how to love you by the way you love yourself. If the people in your life, treated you the way you treat yourself, how would you be treated?

Please understand that no one can complete you. No one can bring you happiness unless you are happy within. No one will make you feel beautiful if you don't see your own beauty. Think about people who never accept a compliment. No matter how many compliments they get, they still find a way to disagree and talk down on themselves.

Take the compliment even when you don't feel pretty. Accept help even if your pride tells you to say no. Go to the party even if you don't like your outfit. Celebrate yourself even when no one else is doing so. Take yourself on dates. Compliment yourself.

Stop and breathe. Embrace the moments. Do what makes you feel free and alive! Forgive yourself. Pamper yourself. Just love yourself! Be the friend you want. Be the partner you're looking for. And most importantly be you, love you, authentically and unapologetically.

Affirm:
I am learning to love myself in the purest form.
I am learning to cheer myself on even when there's no one else in the bleachers.
I am learning to forgive myself & others for what was deemed unforgivable.
I am unlearning what success should look like.
I am unlearning what happiness should look like.
I am learning, unlearning & healing.

What is one thing that you seek from others that you haven't given yourself?

_____
_____
_____
_____
_____
_____
_____
_____
_____
_____

Give yourself 5 compliments that do not pertain to your appearance.

1. _____
2. _____
3. _____
4. _____
5. _____

Affirm:
I promise to love myself like I want to be loved
I am a work of art.
I am beautiful and unique.
I am strong, capable and determined.
I am loved, eloquent & phenomenal.

Self-Care

Self-care is a manifestation of self-love. When we truly love ourselves, we engage in activities to spend time with, love on and attend to ourselves. Self-care is the care you give that caters to your health as a whole. Self-care keeps you healthy and happy enough to to keep going in life. Its catering to your desires and your purpose in life.

A list of self-care activities:

- Getting a massage
- Taking a shower
- Pampering yourself
- Exercising
- Soaking up some sun
- Meditation
- Reading
- Going to therapy
- Journaling
- Consistent doctor appointments
- Keeping a balanced diet

An example of Self-care routine:

- Starting every morning with prayer, and meditation.
- Mondays and Wednesdays, attend yoga class.
- Tuesdays, go to the beach.
- Self-care Sundays consists of washing my hair, cleaning the house, and getting my nails done or getting massages.

How often do you make time for yourself?

What do you usually do in this time?

Plan a self-care day below.

How do you currently start your day?

_____
_____
_____
_____
_____
_____
_____
_____

What you do first thing in the morning will set the tone for your day. The best way to start your day is with a combination of prayer, meditation, exercise, positive thinking and manifestations.

Set a morning routine below.

_____
_____
_____
_____
_____
_____
_____
_____
_____
_____
_____

What does being productive look like to you?

Taking a break or a nap can be considered being productive. Going out with friends can be considered as being productive. We all deserve and need moments to unwind, relax and have fun. If it is benefiting your mental, physical, emotional or financial health, it is considered productive for you.

___

List some self-care activities that you can implement in your regular schedule that do not require money.

For example: washing your hair or writing in your gratitude journal

Plan a vacation below. Then plan to enjoy it! Which locations are you considering? Which dates? What activities do you want to engage in? What do you need to make this vacation a reality. *(reservation, outfits, etc)?*

List 10 things you are grateful for.

1. _____
2. _____
3. _____
4. _____
5. _____
6. _____
7. _____
8. _____
9. _____
10. _____

Do you feel the most gratitude when you give or receive?

_____
_____
_____
_____
_____
_____
_____
_____
_____
_____
_____
_____

It's not about how much we give, but how much love we put into giving.

Name 10 things that make you smile

1. _____
2. _____
3. _____
4. _____
5. _____
6. _____
7. _____
8. _____
9. _____
10. _____

What does the term *pay it forward* mean to you?

_____
_____
_____
_____
_____
_____
_____
_____
_____
_____
_____
_____
_____

In what ways do you give back? If you are not actively giving back right now, make a list of ways you can give back to your community, city, country or even to schools you previously attended.

What is the best gift you've ever received?

Why did this specific gift make such an impact?

Lessons and Thoughts

How are you feeling today? Is anything weighing on your heart? Release it below in the form of a prayer, poem or simply writing it out the way it flows in your mind.

Checking In...

How are you feeling today? Is anything weighing on your heart? Release it below in the form of a prayer, poem or simply writing it out the way it flows in your mind.

CHAPTER 11

Coping Skills

Life is not perfect. Learning how to implement healthy coping skills when we face obstacles will help you become resilient. You'll learn how to manage stress and whether we realize it or not, we all use different strategies to cope. It's natural. Once something occurs, as humans we respond and react. It is no different when negative events occur.

Not sure what your coping skills are? Let's think about it. When you are angry, sad, embarrassed, scared, lonely or experiencing another negative emotion, what do you do? What do you say? What do you avoid doing? Where do you go? If I were to ask your partner, parent or closest friend, how would they say you respond when you are going through a tough situation? These questions will lead you into a thinking process about your coping skills.

Now that you have some ideas of your natural coping skills, let's examine whether they are healthy or unhealthy. Healthy coping skills prepare us for true and sustainable healing and growth while unhealthy ones are temporary, ineffective fixes that usually result in more damage to self and others.

Healthy Coping Skills

- Yoga
- Praying
- Dancing, singing or listening to music
- Meditation
- Journaling
- Exercising
- Walking away
- Spending time in nature
- Expressing your feelings

Unhealthy Coping Skills

- Isolation
- Fighting
- Overindulging in anything (for example shopping, alcohol, food etc)
- Catastrophizing
- Ignoring the problem
- Getting revenge
- Sabotaging your goals by procrastinating & scrolling through social media
- Engaging in self-harm behaviors

The good news is that it is possible to unlearn your unhealthy coping skills and start to practice new ones

Things to know...

When you face obstacles in your life, remember that bad things happen to good people and good things happen to bad people every day. It is out of our control.

Remember bad things don't happen because you deserve it.

When plans fail, instead of beating yourself up, reevaluate! New plan!

Feel your emotions!!! Never, ever, ignore your pain. It's okay to take that time for yourself to feel how you feel, just don't stay there.

It doesn't mean you don't deserve good things or that you are destined for failure. It's a bad moment, nothing else. Even when it feels like nothing else can go wrong, I promise you it can better!

Reflect on your positive times during the negative moments.

Do you utilize healthy or unhealthy coping skills? What are they?

_____
_____
_____
_____
_____
_____
_____
_____
_____
_____
_____
_____
_____

How do you release your anger?

_____
_____
_____
_____
_____
_____
_____
_____
_____
_____
_____
_____

How does your anger affect those around you?

What are your takeaways from this chapter? What did you learn? What are your thoughts? Express it below.

_____
_____
_____
_____
_____
_____
_____
_____
_____
_____
_____
_____
_____
_____
_____
_____
_____
_____
_____
_____
_____
_____
_____

Checking In...

How are you feeling today? Is anything weighing on your heart? Release it below in the form of a prayer, poem or simply writing it out the way it flows in your mind.

CHAPTER 12
Staying True To Yourself

Staying true to yourself means staying aligned. Stay aligned with your purpose, passions, and visions.

Let's put this into perspective. Think about losing a friend or a partner. The words *"I miss you"*

Many people don't miss that friend or that ex-partner — they just miss the person they were with them. Maybe you were less fearful. Maybe you were more liberated. Maybe you felt more confident. That's what this is all about. You must learn to do all of this for yourself. Be who you are regardless of who's in the picture.

Ways you can stay true to yourself:
-Remaining honest with yourself and others
-Never dim your light to fit into a crowd.
-Never change your opinion to seek approval from others
-Never allow someone to discourage you.

Are you living your truth? Or are you living a double life?

_____
_____
_____
_____
_____
_____
_____

Build a castle out of the blocks thrown at you.

Who/What do you believe is in control of your life?

Your struggle with authenticity stems from being conditioned to live a lie.

Are you letting things out of your control, control your life?

_____
_____
_____
_____
_____
_____
_____
_____
_____
_____
_____

In what ways are you usually misunderstood?

_____
_____
_____
_____
_____
_____
_____
_____
_____

Be grateful for who you were, who you are and who you're becoming.

What is something very few people know about you?

Are you living or existing?

What are you passionate about?

What is an uncommon belief that you hold?

What is your purpose in life?

What is the most important thing in your life?

What do you love about yourself?

_____
_____
_____
_____
_____
_____
_____
_____
_____
_____
_____
_____
_____
_____

What hobbies do you enjoy partaking in?

_____
_____
_____
_____
_____
_____
_____
_____
_____
_____
_____
_____
_____
_____

Describe yourself in 3 words.

1. _____
2. _____
3. _____

What makes you feel your best?

_____
_____
_____
_____
_____
_____
_____
_____
_____

What are some things that you wish you could change about yourself? List the reason for each one.

_____
_____
_____
_____
_____
_____
_____
_____
_____
_____
_____

What are your religious/non-religious beliefs and why?

_____
_____
_____
_____
_____
_____
_____
_____
_____
_____
_____
_____
_____
_____
_____

What do you like most about your life currently?

_____
_____
_____
_____
_____
_____
_____
_____
_____
_____
_____
_____

Do you lead with your heart or your mind? Why?

Name a song that makes you happy. Write some of your favorite lyrics from this song and go listen to it.

What is the best piece of advice you've ever received? Who gave you this advice?

When are you most confident?

Which appeals to you more: *Doing the right things or doing things right?* In your opinion, what is the difference between the two?

CHAPTER 14

Congratulations! You have reached the end of this journey.

Now, it is time to reflect.

How did this journal help you to make progress in achieving your mental and emotional health goals?

_____
_____
_____
_____
_____
_____
_____
_____
_____
_____
_____
_____
_____
_____
_____
_____
_____
_____
_____

What can you do to continue to progress in these areas?

What was your favorite section of this journal?

What are the biggest lessons that you learned from this journal?

Who is one person who you believe will benefit from getting their own copy of this journal?

Buy it for them or recommend it to them so they can get it for themself!

Epilogue

Working on yourself and taking the necessary steps to heal does not mean your life will become perfect. It just means your journey through life will be perfect. With healing, you'll understand that you're growing through obstacles instead of going through them. You'll understand that everything happens for you and not to you. You'll focus on the lessons and blessings in every situation. Once you understand that, you'll master life.

Although you've completed this book, your work is still not done.

Never forget that healing and growth are continuous. The more we go through life is the more we will learn, unlearn, grow and heal.

As we face new obstacles and experiences, new and old emotions may arise for us to work through. When these emotions arise, do not suppress them. Face them head on.

As you continue to move through life, I wish you all the best. I pray you find the peace and love that you deserve.

I pray you achieve the life your heart desires.

I pray you blossom into the person you aspire to be.

Contact Or Follow-Up With Me:

Email: healing@evernewinnovations.com

Please leave an honest review about your experience with this journal on the site of the retailer in which purchased.

Free Resources

Suicide Prevention Lifeline
1(800) 273-8255

National Sexual Assault Lifeline
1(800) 656-4673

Child Abuse Hotline
1(800) 422-4636

LGBTQ+ Support Line
1(866) 488-7386

National Domestic Violence Hotline
1(800) 799-7233

Teen & Young Adult Support Line
1(800) 872-5437

National HIV/AIDS Hotline
1(800) 232-4636

Crisis Support Via Chat
Text "*ANSWER*" to 839-963
Text "*HOME*" to 741-741
Chat Online at *www.hotline.rainn.org*

End Notes

247 Motivation. (2021, April 13). *Les Brown motivation - Control your emotions (Best Motivational Video)* [Video]. YouTube. https://www.youtube.com/watch?v=Zd1PRsMW8OE&t=544s

Bhatia, M. (2021, May 10). *Confused about credit? So are a lot of people. Let's fix that.* Credit Karma. https://www.creditkarma.com/advice/i/learn-credit-score-factors

Demers, J. (2014, November 3). *51 Quotes to inspire success in your life and business.* Inc. https://www.inc.com/jayson-demers/51-quotes-to-inspire-success-in-your-life-and-business.html

Ernest, C. (2014, September 4). *Why are coping skills so important?* Sunny Sky Counseling. http://www.sunnyskycounseling.com/blog/2014/9/4/why-are-coping-skills-so-important

Griffin, T. (2021, December 7). *How to stay true to yourself* [Online forum post]. wikiHow. https://www.wikihow.com/Stay-True-to-Yourself

Johir, Q. (2019, December 3). *How To Reprogram Subconscious Mind: The one cycle that determines your fate (Dirty Secret)* [Video]. YouTube. https://www.youtube.com/watch?v=FM8_ZfEd9zg&t=123s

IFORHER. (2021, June 4). *40 Oprah Winfrey quotes on life, relationships, success & more.* IFORHER. https://www.iforher.com/quotes/famous-people/oprah-winfrey-quotes-life-relationships-failure-success-confidence-motivational-inspiring-quotes/

Powell, K. (2020, February 12). *50 Questions to ask relatives about family history.* ThoughtCo. https://www.thoughtco.com/fifty-questions-for-family-history-interviews-1420705

Psychology Today. (n.d.). Unconscious. Psychology Today. https://www.psychologytoday.com/us/basics/unconscious

Rudolph, K. (2018, July 3). 5 Reasons why it feels so darn hard to love yourself sometimes. *YourTango*. https://www.yourtango.com/experts/kellyrudolph/5-reasons-hard-to-love-yourself-and-how-to-make-self-love-easier

Wrigley, J. (2020, July 10). What causes codependency? *My Online Therapy*. https://myonlinetherapy.com/what-causes-codependency/

www.ingramcontent.com/pod-product-compliance
Lightning Source LLC
Chambersburg PA
CBHW050805220426
43209CB00088BA/1643